Richard Glover is the author of six books and the stage show, *Lonestar Lemon*. His weekly column has appeared in the *Sydney Morning Herald* since 1985. Richard also presents the Drive show on ABC radio in Sydney.

Also by Richard Glover

Grin and Bear It

The P-Plate Parent
(with Angela Webber)

Laughing Stock

The Joy of Blokes
(with Angela Webber)

In Bed with Jocasta

For children

The Dirt Experiment

the dag's dictionary

very funny
a book of words that
should exist — but don't

richard glover

illustrated by matthew martin

ABC
Books

Published by ABC Books for the
AUSTRALIAN BROADCASTING CORPORATION
GPO Box 9994 Sydney NSW 2001

First published August 2004

National Library of Australia
Cataloguing-in-Publication data.
Glover, Richard.
The dag's dictionary : a very funny book of words
that should exist, but don't.
ISBN 0 7333 1436 8.
1. Wit and humor. 2. English language – New words –
Dictionaries. 3. English language – New words – Humor.
I. Australian Broadcasting Corporation. II. Title.
423.310207

Illustrations by Matthew Martin
Cover and internal design by Christabella Designs
Set in 12/15pt Sabon by Kirby Jones
Colour reproduction by PageSet, Melbourne
Printed and bound in Australia by
McPherson's Printing Group, Victoria

5 4 3 2 1

Introduction

The people who write dictionaries are terrible hoarders — they can't bring themselves to throw anything out. Flip through the *Macquarie*, the *Oxford* or the *Collins* and you constantly find yourself wandering through the backstreets of medieval England. A 'liripoop', I discovered during a flip just then, is defined as the dangling extension on a medieval hood. It's a great-sounding word. Now all I've got to do is work out a way of dropping it into casual conversation.

Similarly, 'buskins' (laced sandals), a 'firkin' (a unit of measurement), and for that matter a 'merkin' (a pubic wig). Maybe I'm hanging out with a dull crowd, but I now find myself going months on end without spotting a single pubic wig. (And even when you do it's considered polite not to mention it.)

Meanwhile, the dictionaries are silent on a whole series of modern experiences. I may no longer need a word to describe the strange pockmarks left on the skin by the bubonic plague, but I certainly need a word for the lewd and crazy dance I find myself doing whenever I'm alone in an elevator.

What do you call the irresistible urge to pop the plastic bubbles in bubble wrap? Or the city slicker who dresses in moleskins and an Akubra hat? And what about the group of smokers clustered around the entrance to an office building?

About fifty of the words in this book were created by listeners to *Drive* on ABC radio, who enthusiastically took up the challenge of spotting holes in the language, and then finding the perfect word to fill them.

The other 300 or so were created in my own word foundry at home, amid the bliss of the suburbs. Creating new words involves a fair bit of noise — swearing, stomping about, rhyming, punning, drinking heavily and other unattractive behaviour. I need to thank my family, and my neighbours. Perhaps they just wanted the bloody book to be finished, but towards the end they even started making contributions. Sometimes it was to supply a word for a spare definition I had lying around on the workshop floor; other times to throw another definition into the pile.

Thanks especially to my son Joe Glover, without whom we may never have discovered the word for those underpants designed to be worn with the brand name showing; to my friends Rene Vogelzang and Jurate Janavicius, Lynne and Edgar Downes, Lucy Bell, Tony Horwitz and Geraldine Brooks, and, of course, my partner Debra Oswald.

Thanks also to my radio colleagues, especially Jo Chichester, James O'Loghlin, James Valentine, Robyn Ball, Jodie Maguire and Sascha Rundle, and to Brigitta Doyle and Kate Pollard from ABC Books.

This may look like a dictionary, but what it's really about is the weird rituals and experiences of modern life. I hope you'll recognise yourself somewhere in these pages, and that you'll forgive me for letting our shared secrets out of the bag.

So give your liripoop a tug and carefully position your merkin. We're off on a journey of Dagscovery.

Aa

Abbacadabra
(ab ba' kad a bra) n.
The phenomenon whereby an Abba song miraculously appears in every Australian movie.

Abdomino effect
(ab' do mi noe ef ekt) n.
Descriptive of the way a group of male friends gradually gets fatter, as each bloke in turn lets himself go.

Ad nausea
(ad nor' zia) n.
When watching the crickct on TV, the feeling you get after having seen twenty-three ads in a row during the lunch break.

Airfauxbics

(ayr' fo biks) n.
Any sequence of stretching exercises designed to cover the fact that the person at whom you just waved turned out to be a complete stranger.

Alphabutt

(al fa' but) n.
In the entertainment industry, the superior status given to the singer with the best bottom, currently Kylie Minogue.

Alphamumble

(al fa' mum ble) v.

To surreptitiously run though the alphabet when using the phone book, in order to remember exactly where 'R' comes.

Ambidisastrous

(am bih de zars' trus) adj.

In football, to be equally incompetent with either foot.

Anecdultery

(an nek dul tah ree) n.

The moment when you are halfway through telling someone a story — acting in the know and exaggerating like crazy — when you realise it was their story in the first place.

Dagword by Greg Wall. Also: Communitake (Sophie Braham); and Theminiscing (Neil Elleson).

Aquadakstrous

(ak wah dak' strus) adj.

Descriptive of the tendency for water to splash onto the front of a man's trousers when he's washing his hands, causing everyone to assume he's got bladder-control issues.

Aquakinesis

(ak wha kee nee' sus) n.

The ability of a spoon to move itself directly under the tap in the sink, thus ensuring a spray of water over anybody who turns on the tap.

Artnosticism

(art nos' tee cizm) n.

The moment, in a modern art gallery, when you feel unable to say whether the thing in front of you is a work of art or part of the air-conditioning system.

Artnosticism

Auntiediluvian

(arn tee' di loo' vee an) adj.

Pertaining to the fierce views about the likelihood of sudden rain and the need to take a warm jacket, as expressed by female relatives.

Austintation

(os tin' tay shun) n.

The practice, common among ten-year-old boys, of constantly showing off how they can do the voice from Austin Powers.

Autopia

(or toe' pee ah) n.

The sense of joy and elation when you find a vacant parking space right outside the place you need to go.

Dagword by Clodagh O'Grady from a definition by James Hocking. Also: Glee-spot (Dian Sadler); Parkindipity (Chris Gow); Carphoria (Maureen Delves); Sedan-dipity (Paddy Mullin). Phrases: Carparke diem — literally 'quick, seize the space' (Ken Gill).

Autopology

(or' toe poh loh' gee) n.
The grimace of apology and regret you give to another motorist after doing something truly stupid.

Avoiddance

(ah voy' dans) n.
The process of stepping sharply to the left, and then the left again, and then back down the street, when you want to avoid someone at the shops.

Bb

Bacontrite
(bay kon' tryt) adj.
Feeling regretful and full of self-reproach twenty minutes after eating a full English breakfast.

Barbequeue
(bar be' cue) n.
The line of blokes at a BBQ telling the host when to turn the chops, and trying to get a go at the tongs.

Batbiter
(bat' by tah) n.
A cricketer who, having swung at the ball and missed, takes a good hard look at his bat, as if the reason for the failure must lie therein.

Bedinage
(bed' in ayg) n.
Playful repartee or banter between two blokes on the subject of their amazing success with the opposite sex.

Bellwilderment
(bel wil' da ment) n.
The moment of communal panic when a mobile phone rings and everyone assumes it's theirs.

Bellyquake
(bell ee' kwayk) n.
A rumbling in the stomach that produces strange and alarming sounds, most commonly at moments of great importance.

Bellyvent
(bell ee' vent) n.
The open gap of fabric between the buttons on a fat man's shirt.

Benchquet
(bench' kwet) n.

A second or third helping of dinner, eaten straight from the pot while standing at the kitchen bench, in the belief that calories consumed in this way don't count.

Bigobbling
(by' gob ling) v.

The practice of refusing to take the last bit of cheese or cake, so as not to appear greedy, and instead cutting it in half, eating that, then cutting it in half again, and eating that, until there is a tiny sliver which you then gulp down because, 'There's only a little bit left and someone's got to eat it.'

Billge
(bilj) n.

The pile of unpaid bills, school excursion permission forms and council leaflets that accumulate on the corner of the kitchen bench or somewhere in the hallway.

Binfidel

(bin' fid elle) n.

A person who sneaks his rubbish into your wheelie bin once it's been put out on the kerb, so there's never any space for your last forgotten bag.

Dagword by Steve Harop from a definition by John Stackhouse. Also: Sulo-path (Mark Cossins); Garbitrageur (Robert Cooper); Binfilltrator (Christopher Millhouse); Coup d'etatrash (Howard Bayliss); Binboozler (Evelyn Saunders); Binposter (Nicole Anthony); and, Richard's suggestion, Osama Bin Loader. The person whose bin is thus misused is, of course, a Muckold (Jesse Wynhausen).

Blabvertising

(blab' ver ty zing) n.

The announcement of your imminent arrival, via a mobile phone call, minutes, or sometimes seconds, before you actually arrive.

Blameboozled
(blaym' boo zuld) adj.
So adept at blaming other people for your failings, you've even convinced yourself.

Blinkocrat
(blink' o krat) n.
A motorist who believes he can park anywhere, however absurd or disruptive, providing he turns on his hazard lights.

Blokeade
(blowk' ayd) n.
The impassable wedge of men surrounding the beer and food at any party. By extension, the impassable wedge of men surrounding the top jobs in any organisation.

Bluffoon

(bluf' oon) n.

A person who makes such unlikely boasts about his or her own achievements that everyone instantly knows it's all lies.

Boaggerise

(bow' agg ahr' eyes) v.

To injure one's hand when trying to open a bottle of yuppie beer in the mistaken belief it's twist-top.

Boastbuster

(bowst' bus tah) n.

A person who, when asked to guess how cheaply you bought something, or the size of your pay rise at work, always picks a figure so extreme that your excellent story falls completely flat.

Dagword by Lea Kirkwood. Also: Overguesstimator (Sylvia Monsted); Anecdope (Rupert Smoker); and Pestimator (Justin O'Connell).

Bonnet-apnoea

(bon it' ap nee' ah) n.

A sleeping disease that overcomes men when forced to watch BBC bonnet dramas.

Bon not

(bon' not) n.

The witty response that comes to mind thirty minutes after an unexpected jibe has left you lost for words.

Dagword by Julie Silk from a definition by Geoff Donnellan. Also: Hindslight (François McHardy); Retalilate (John Lewis); Laughterthought (Stephanie Wallbank); and, Richard's suggestion, a Waiticism.

Boohoography

(boo hoo' og ra fee) n.

A political memoir in which the author laments over his or her career, blaming others for each and every disaster.

Bookblister

(book' blih stah) n.

The bubble of trapped air that's impossible to avoid when covering school books with sticky plastic.

Boomerwrong

(boo mah' rong) n.

A boomerang that won't come back; a stick.

Borecaster

(baw' kah stah) n.

The guy in front of you at the football or cricket who knows more about the game than anybody else — and insists on loudly sharing his every theory.

Boredacious

(baw day' shus) adj.

Recklessly bold in the choice of an anecdote heard by the gathered company many, many times before.

Botax rate

(bow taks' rayt) n.

The percentage of expression lost by those who've had botox injections.

Bragpiper

(brahg' py pah) n.

A person who tells you about their achievements non-stop, without even drawing breath, using a circular breathing technique borrowed from those who play the bagpipes.

Bragtag

(brahg' tahg) n.

A car bumper sticker that points out the name of the school one's kids attend, the profession one is a member of, or the upmarket sport in which one participates — in the hope of impressing the rest of the world with one's social standing.

Dagword by Sally Sweeny. Also: Posevert (Brian Lutman); Boastage stamp (Jo Hubble); Narcisssticker (David Murray); MEtag (Jenny Lowe); and Haughtograph (Walter de Jong).

Brick teaser

(brik' tee zah) n.

A person who goes to 'open for inspection' houses with absolutely no intention of buying, but merely to have a stickybeak.

Dagword by Tim Miles from a definition by Kate Young. Also: Buypasser (Barbara Maher); Brick kicker (Lisa McCutchion); Squizitor (Mark Cossins); and Maison d'etres (Christine Southcombe). Phrases: Fake and enterer (Julie Ellis); and an LJ Havelooker (Miles Oakley).

Brietentious

(bree' ten shus) adj.
Descriptive of a person who shows off
about cheese.

Bro-kart
(bro' kaht) n.
A car jam-packed with young men, with the CD player turned up to 11.

Bubble-wrapture
(buh bul' rap cha) n.
The irresistible urge to pop the plastic bubbles in bubble wrap.

Buckstop
(buhk' stop) n.
The space left between the person using an automatic teller machine and the first person in the queue behind them.

Dagword by Geoff Warren from a definition by Ben Greentree. Also: Tellermoat (Vincent Caruana); PINformation gap (Diane Sadler); PIN cushion (Rob Deep); and Dough man's land (Sharon Green).

Bumbaker

(bum' bay' kah) n.

A person who has sat in the same office chair for too long, causing it to overheat.

Bumbilical cord

(bum' bil i' kuhl cawd) n.

The fixed connection between two teenage lovers walking with their hands in each other's back pocket.

Bunterise

(bun' tah ryz) v.

To accessorise yourself with full-figured friends in the hope that they'll make you look thin.

Bun voyage

(bun' voy arj)

A phrase used to farewell your hamburger meat as it slips from your bun towards the floor.

Bussa nova

(bus ah' no' vah) n.

The wild dance first forward and then backwards, performed by standing passengers when the bus comes to a sudden halt.

Buttle

(but' uhl) v.

To tug constantly at the back of one's low-cut jeans in a vain attempt to pull them up to some sort of decent and comfortable height.

Cc

Cadamite
(kah dah' myt) n.
A woman who's always attracted to the worst bloke in the room.

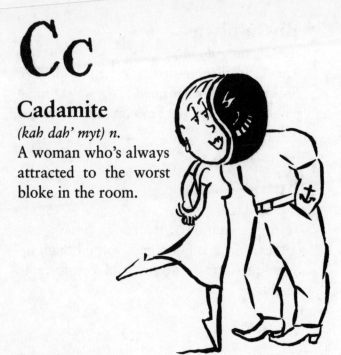

Callamity
(kawl' ah mah' tee) n.
The long, embarrassing message you just left on someone's answering machine, so embarrassing you think you may well have to burn down their house, rather than have them hear it.

Carbarian

(cah beh' ri un) n.

A motorist who accelerates from the traffic lights as if it's the start of a major military offensive.

Carte blanch

(kart' blanch) v.

To become suddenly pale as a result of opening a restaurant menu and seeing the prices.

Catasonic

(kat' ah son ik) adj.

The speed at which a cat moves after you tread on its tail.

Catcent

(kat' sent) n.

The ridiculous, childlike voice used in cat food advertisements, in which a cat supposedly endorses the product.

Cause celebra

(kors' selay brah) n.

The feeling of immense relief when a man, operating single-handedly and in the dark, finally manages to unhook a bra.

CDecoy

(see dee' koy) n.

The groovy CD placed on top of the pile of daggy ones when you've got someone to impress.

Cellulights

(sell' u lyts) n.

The especially harsh lights found in fashion-shop changing rooms designed to prove you must cover your body at all times, preferably with their overpriced clothes.

Charlaturn

(shah lah' tern) v.

The practice, among motorists, of only turning on their indicator to turn right once the lights have changed to green.

Dagword by Jenny Lowe from a definition by Robyn Jordan. Also: Turnpiker (Andrew Jarvis); Nindicator (Rebecca Horner); Procrasturnator (Sally Conrick); and, of course, Volvo Driver (Ken Willis).

Chatatonic

(kat' a ton ik) adj.

Descriptive of a stuporous state achieved after a long period on the phone to a friend who just won't shut up.

Chat-nap

(chat' nap) v.

To daydream while your spouse is talking to you, the idyll ending with a sudden pause and the realisation you've been asked a question but have no idea what it was. You do, however, realise you are in big trouble.

Dagword by Steve Harop from a definition by Fraser Murray. Also: Deaf knell (Julie Ellis); Manopause (Mark Rhodes); Manesia (Sanjaya Senanayake); Chatolepsy (Max Moore); and Whoops-a-daze (Lee Khan).

Cheapuccino

(chi puh' chi no) n.

A cappuccino, as made in rural Australia, with frothy milk and instant coffee.

Cinearse

(sin e' ars) n.

The aching bum you get when watching a long European film.

Clarifart

(kla ri' faht) v.

To move your bum on a vinyl office chair or leather couch in order to produce yet another farting sound, so that everyone might understand that the first alarming noise, produced a moment ago, was not an actual fart.

Dagword by Sean Mooney. Also: Fakeulence (Paul Spence); Plastulence (Chris Whitehall); and Bumtriloquism (Cath O'Regan).

Cleptopainiac

(klep toe' pay' nee ak) n.

A person who, when you confess a headache or other illness, claims the same affliction — only ten times worse.

Coach potato

(kowch' pot ay' toh) n.

A sports fan, usually a man, who lies on the couch in front of the TV shouting instructions to the players in the apparent belief they can hear what he's saying.

Coinstipated

(koyn' stee pay tid) adj.

Descriptive of the miserly rich, who earn millions, but can never find the shrapnel for a cup of coffee.

Confidon't

(kon' fee don't) n.

A friend who blurts out all your secrets.

Copcaranoia

(kop kah' rah noy ah) n.

The guilty feeling that comes over you the instant you see a police car in the rear-view mirror, even though you've done nothing wrong.

Cordon blur

(kaw don' bluh) n.

The moment, halfway through cooking a recipe, when you blindly add a tablespoon of cayenne pepper instead of the required pinch.

Correctus interruptus

(koh rec tus' in tah rup' tus) n.

While travelling on public transport, the irresistible urge to answer a question, or even to correct a fact, in an overheard conversation.

Dagword by Sarah McCoy from a definition by Jane May.
Also: Encyclopedantry (Ralph Horner); Busyboffining
(Owen Heldon); Quote-us interrupt-us (Francesca Muir);
and Lipo-friction (Lianna Taranto).

Corridoroboree

(koh ree daw' rob oh ree) n.

The strange dance that occurs when two people are trying to pass in a corridor, characterised by the couple stepping left, then right, then left again in a failed effort to get past each other.

Dagword by John Darcy. Also: Spar de deux (Ern Crocker); Pass de deux (Kaye Russell); and Teeterbugging (Jenny Lowe).

Cosmetic perjury

(koz met ik' pur jah ree) n.

The tactful response required when you meet an acquaintance who has proudly changed their hair, face or body in a failed attempt to improve their appearance.

Dagword by Allan Cropper from a definition by Greg Webster. Also: Compliement (Liz O'Hare); Fake-lift (Brett Wright); Umdiscretion (Chris Cunliffe-Jones); and Liarlogue (Laurie Allison).

Costentatious

(kos ten tay' shus) adj.
Leaving a price tag on a present 'by mistake'
so everyone will know how much it cost.

Costigate

(kos' tee gayt) v.
To criticise your partner for overspending,
especially on clothes or wine.

Coup de grass

(koo' de grass) n.
The act of concreting-over all your lawn so
you never have to mow the bastard again.

Crap-trap

(krap' trap) n.
The drawer in which you keep all the home-
delivery food menus.

Critterbugging

(krit ah' bug ing) n.

The frantic dance executed after you accidentally walk through a spider's web.

Dagword by Garth Clarke from a definition by Richard Bandler. Also: Fang-dango (Mark Gordon); Cobweboree (Barbara Maher); Damnbada (Mike Hluchan); Arach 'n' roll (Hester Walter); Whirl-while-webbed (Jan Waddington); Mackarackeena (Michael Kennedy); Webbing dervish (Carol Ferguson); and Spun doubt ballet (Brian and Vicki Benson).

Cybore

(sy' baaw) n.

Someone who tells you more than you want to know about their computer and its number of bytes.

Cyclopath

(sy klo' path) n.

An angry, self-righteous man wearing tight lycra bike shorts, scattering children and dogs as he exercises both himself and his rights.

Dd

Dadulation
(dad' you lay' shun) n.
The extravagant praise expected by men
who have completed a domestic task.

Dagmology

(dag' mol o gee) n.
The study of Dagwords, their discovery and spread.

Dagosaurus

(dag o' saw rus) n.
A dictionary of Dagwords and their synonyms.

Dagster

(dag' stah) n.
A person who creages Dagwords. See also Laxicographer.

Dagword

(dag' wurd) n.
A word that fills a gap in the language.

Damn!nesia

(damn nee' zee ah) n.

An affliction by which you walk purposefully from one end of the building to the other, but forget mid-trip where you were going.

Dagword by Richard Murnane. Also: Aimnesia (Timothy Hunter); and Alzambulate (Warren Berkery).

Dawntankerous

(dorn tan' kah rus) adj.

Feeling bad-tempered as a result of being woken up at five in the morning by the noise from next door.

Decorotation

(de k or' row tay' shun) n.

The art of moving around your furniture in order to cover up the latest wine spill.

Deja-news

(day jah' newz) n.

News footage that flashes up during a movie recorded off the TV five years ago, which nonetheless seems perfectly up to date.

Deja-Woo

(day jah' woo) n.

The latest action picture from Hollywood's John Woo, which is always inexplicably similar to the last one.

Derrnouement

(der nu' ment) n.

The moment in any movie when the main character chooses to do something amazingly stupid and dangerous to bring the plot to a conclusion.

Derrpositary

(der poz' i tuh ree) n.

A hiding place chosen for some particularly crucial item that's so clever and so unexpected, you now can't remember it yourself.

Derrtective

(der tek' tiv) n.

The slow-witted police officer who just can't manage to capture the criminals in a heist movie.

Derr titles
(der' ty tuls) n.
The superimposed words on the *Jerry Springer* show that explain the situation for those who find the interview too complex to follow, as in, 'Believes He is a Lesbian', or 'Has Married His Own Dog'.

Dialiloquy
(dy uhl' il oh kwee) n.
A message to oneself, left on one's own answering machine as a reminder to do something, which is delivered in a strangely intimate and loving voice.

Didgeridoodles
(did juh' ree doo' duhls) n.
The meaningless decorations along the surface of a made-in-China tourist-shop didgeridoo.

Digger mortis

(di gah' maw tis) n.

An affliction suffered by council road crews, whereby they appear to be leaning on their shovels, but have in fact died at some point during the day.

Dinkhana

(din' kah nah) n.
The competition between two rev-heads over whose car engine can make the most noise.

Dinstant

(din' stant) n.
The time period between the traffic lights turning green, and the sound of the car horn beeping behind you.

Dagword by Craig Brown from a definition by Jeff Scott. Also: Spit-second (Alison Hartwell); and The blink-of-an-ire (Christina Bodiroza).

Dipthong

(dip' thong) n.
The worn-down bit on the heel of a rubber thong that makes it easier to make a fast turn for the fish and chip shop.

Direlogue

(dy ah' log) n.
The heavily scripted 'banter' between the male and female hosts during an awards night telecast.

Dittocism

(dit oh' siz um) n.
A joke that you told your friend last week, and which he or she is now repeating back to you, as if it were freshly minted.

Dittographer

(dit oh' gra fah) n.
Someone who claims 'exactly the same thing happened to me', just so they can take over the conversation and make it all about themselves.

Doojitsu

(doo jit' su) n.

The flurry of choreographed arm movements required to put a doona into a doona cover. As in all martial arts, the outcome is uncertain, with victory often going to the doona.

Doonarism

(doo nah' riz um) n.
The transposition of a doona, whereby it is now going across the bed, with your feet sticking out the bottom.

Doorgasm

(daw' gaz um) n.
The flood of sudden elation experienced when the doorman at a trendy club finally lets you in.

Doppelklanger

(dop ul' klang ah) n.
The moment when you spot Burt Newton, Rove, or the girl from the Woolies ad in the street, and mistake them for a personal friend.

Dorkscrew

(dawk' skru) n.

A show-off corkscrew featuring several strange handles, levers and pneumatic functions, which costs ten times more than the bottle it's opening.

Dreadlock

(dred' lok) n.

At the cinema, the imaginary brake, located within the armrests, which you squeeze when the action gets too exciting.

Dream spleen

(dreem spleen) n.

The irrational grudge you hold against someone who was mean to you during a dream.

Dorkscrew

Dresstitute

(dres' tee tyoot) adj.

Descriptive of a woman when she looks into her crowded wardrobe and realises she has nothing, absolutely nothing, to wear.

Driptease

(drip' teez) n.

The splash of liquid left in a bottle by a lazy housemate so that it may be returned to the fridge, thus saving the person the effort of washing it or recycling it.

Dagword by Andrew Newman from a definition by Paul Davis. Also: Annoyounce (Nellie Evans); Laterade (Michael Kennedy); Sweinlager (Mike Hluchan); and Slackdash (Joseph Lee).

Droodle

(dru' dul) n.

A small puddle of drool, which deposits itself on the front of one's shirt during an afternoon doze.

Dudmentia

(dud men' cha) n.

A woman's ability to forget how rotten all her past boyfriends turned out to be, so as to be able to fall in love with the next.

Ee

Earternity
(ee ah' ter ni tee) n.
That endless and peculiarly enervating period
of time when you are stuck holding the phone
to your ear, waiting for your bank, Internet
company or insurer to actually attend to you.

*Dagword by Nicole Anthony from a definition by Ingrid
Mogensen. Also: Holdathon (Alan Smith); Teledium
(Robert Cooper); and Hellhold (Kate McLean).*

Edgehog
(edj' hog) n.
A person who hogs the aisle seat in a train
so that you have to climb over them to get
to a vacant spot.

*Dagword by Mark Rhodes from a definition by Phin Tjhai.
Also: Greedhump (Shaun McFayden); Scuseknee (Diana
Cantrell); Yobstacle (Frank Williams); AisleBeRightMate
(David Morris); Aislander (Ken Gill); a Knobsticle
(Maurice Hanna); and Aisleywacker (Susan Anthony).*

Eelation

(ee' lay shun) n.

The feeling of excitement when you turn on your home computer and discover you have twenty e-mails in your inbox.

Eespondent

(ee' spon dent) n.

The disappointment that follows when you discover all twenty e-mails have the subject line, 'Do You Want A Bigger Penis?'

Eesurance

(ee' shaw rants) n.

The tendency of middle management to forward all possible e-mails to their staff so that, in case of trouble, they can blame the underlings for 'never reading their e-mails'.

Eetritus

(ee' try tus) n.

The disgusting detritus that falls out when you tip your computer keyboard upside down.

Eggistentialist

(egg' is ten shul ist) n.

A person who doesn't care whether the chicken came before the egg, or vice versa, since the world is essentially absurd and unknowable.

Eggsbestos

(egg zbes' dos) n.

The crispy thatch of white under a fried egg that's been cooked too fast.

Enigmartyred

(en nyg' mar tahd) adj.

Consistently attracted by silent, brooding types, only to discover that they've usually got nothing to say.

Eskyvate

(es kee' vayt) v.

To dig downwards in an Esky in order to uncover the very last can of cold beer.

Eskyvate

Eviangelist

(eh vee ahn' gee lyst) n.

A person who believes, somewhat mystically, that they can stop dogs and cats weeing on their front lawn by littering it with plastic drink bottles.

Dagword by Denise Cook-Parker. Also: Piss-de-resistancers (Norm Berry); Pissimist (Ken Paton); and a Ground poobar (Kath O'Connor).

Eyesberg

(eyz' burg) n.

The icy look a teenage boy gives his mother when he wants her to stop talking to his girlfriend.

Dagword by Barbara Maher from a definition by Angela Bradshaw. Also: Off-peek (Jack Herman); Eyescream (Annette Henderson); Elderwince (Maurice Oliver); and Frigidglare (Nerida White).

Ff

Fabrican't
(fab' ri kant) n.
The white lie you tell when you are invited
to a party and don't want to go, but can't
bring yourself to say a simple 'no thank
you'.

*Dagword by Dennis White from a definition by Glenda
Birch. Also: Can'tomime (Matthew O'Dempsey); Anifonly
(Russell Edwards); and Fibrication (Carol Ferguson).*

Falsifatify
(fal see' fat ee' fy) v.
To place a fat-free label on a product that
never contained fat anyway, such as a
packet of salt or a bottle of cordial, in order
to fool the overly optimistic.

Famnesia

(fam nee' zee ah) n.

The tendency to mix up the names of family members, calling the boy by the girl's name, the father by the mother's, and the baby girl by the dog's.

Fantarctica

(fan' tahk tik ah) n.

The cold, icy emptiness experienced by a former celebrity once their fans have all moved on.

Fartastrophe

(fah tas' trah fee) n.

The loud fart that arrives with no warning at the worst possible time, normally in front of a large audience, or a prospective lover.

Faultageist

(folt' ah guyst) n.

A mechanical problem that disappears as soon as you are in the presence of an expert, making you look like a complete idiot. The machine, of course, goes bung again as soon as the expert leaves.

Dagword by Anton Reich from a definition by Christopher Knox. Also: Polterglitch (Jenny Lowe); and Shremlin (Andrew Parken).

Fartastrophe

Faultimatum

(folt' ee may' tum) n.

The point in every marriage where one person is told they have to admit they were wrong — or else.

Fauxcabulary

(fo' kab yu' ler ee) n.

A series of words used for the sole purpose of making yourself sound modish, groovy or intelligent.

Fauxcrastination

(fo' kras tin ay shun) n.

The shy Australian art of bargaining, in which you pretend you can't make your mind up in the hope the store keeper will take pity and offer a discount.

Feng shoey

(feng' shoo ee) n.
The ancient male practice of abandoning at least one pair of shoes in every room in the house, in order to maximise his own energy flow.

Fixulator

(fiks' yu lay tah) n.
A person who always starts projects around the house but never finishes them.

Dagword by Tony Reynolds from a definition by Grant Moran. Also: Gunnavator (Ray Millar); Renolater (Brendan Russell-Cooper); Gunnadoo (Marian Aitken); Soonsayer (Tony Hunt); Fibricator (Mary Werkhoven); Delaybourer (Barbara Maher); When-o-vator (Evelyn Saunders); and Gavin (Gavin's wife). Phrases: Slack of all trades (Jane Park); He of the never never (Fiona Landgren).

Flamingo Yoga

(flah min go' yo' ga) n.
The practice of washing one's feet under the shower by standing on one foot, while tucking the other, sole upwards, on one's thigh.

Flaparazzi

Flaparazzi

(fla pah' rah tzee) n.

The person who is always in the background of a live news report, waving stupidly at the camera.

Dagword by Ken Gill from a definition by Sally Price. Also: Telepathetics (Fraser Murray); Vextra (Ralph Horner); Sadvert (HuiLing Sun); Hameo (Steve Hogg); Extrabitionist (David John); and Eyejacker (Kerry Murray). Phrases: An Embedded journopest (Richard Murnane); a Stalking head (Alan Smith).

Floop

(flewp) n.

A pile of unlabelled floppy discs that can never be thrown out, just in case one of them proves to contain something important.

Forgiftfulness

(faw gift' ful nes) n.

The practice of buying the perfect Christmas present in September and then forgetting where you hid it.

Four-wheel-drivel
(faw' weel' driv uhl) n.

The stream of excuses that four-wheel-drive owners now feel obliged to offer as explanation for why they own one, despite living in the city.

Fridgebit
(fridj' bit) n.

Food that contains no calories by virtue of being eaten straight from the fridge, while standing with the door of the fridge still open and the light spilling out.

Fumimates
(fu' me mayts) n.

The groups of smokers clustered around the entrance to an office building.

Fumimates

Gg

Gabkhana
(gab' kah nah) n.
Among seven year olds, the happy sport of debating the rules of a new game for so long that they never get to play it.

Gesundblight
(gez und' blyt) n.
The affliction of allowing a tissue to smuggle itself into the wash, resulting in the spread of white fluff onto everything in the machine.

Gesundwhites
(gez und' wyts) n.
The white fluff itself.

Gizmoseum
(giz mo' zee um) n.
In the kitchen, the second or third drawer down, which contains every utensil and implement that is rarely, if ever, used.

Dagword by Jenny Lowe from a definition by Nellie Evans. Also: Nicknacknook (Denise Jones); and The hoardin pavilion (Richard Murnane).

Glitzkrieg
(glits' kreeg) n.
The sudden arrival of the fashionable set at a Sydney party, usually followed by their rapid onward movement.

Gluedini

Gluedini
(gloo' dee ni) n.
A person who, having just used superglue, finds all his fingers are stuck together, and he must now try to escape.

Go-blivious
(glo' bliv ee us) adj.
Descriptive of a dinner guest who is ignoring your hints that it's time to go home, even when you start turning the lights on and off, and saying 'Time, gentlemen, please'.

Gone vivant
(gon vee' vant) n.
A good-time boy who has passed his prime.

Gooffaw
(goo' faw) n.
A knowing chuckle designed to cover up the fact that you didn't get a joke, despite being in a roomful of people who did.

Grating

(gray' ting) n.

The tight, grim smile given to someone you pass for the fourth time in ten minutes in the office corridor, the first three meetings having already exhausted the 'Good morning', 'Working hard!', and the hilarious 'We must stop meeting like this'.

Grogambulate

(grog' am byu' layt) v.

To walk with excessive attention to posture and carriage when drunk but trying to act sober.

Guacamêlée
(gwok ah' mel ay) n.
The riotous surge of party goers towards the dips and biscuits at the start of a function.

Guylingual
(guy' lin gwal) adj.
Descriptive of an Australian woman who can take part in a conversation about cars, football and chundering.

Hh

Haka-ventilate

(ha ka' ven' til ayt) v.
To cool down a piece of food once it's in your mouth by panting, waving and making your eyes bulge.

Hatmosphere

(hat' mus fere) n.
The build-up of heat and sweat that forms beneath the rim of a baseball cap.

Haughtyculturalist

(haw tee' cul chah' rul ist) n.
A person who insists on using the proper Latin names for all his plants.

Hawkestra

(haw kes' tra) n.
The choir of coughers, sneezers and hawkers who spend their lives attending classical music concerts and plays.

Hementia

(he men' shuh) n.
A disease affecting men, whereby each and every morning they forget where they left their car keys.

Hexpiration

(heks' pir ay' shun) n.
The tendency for a product to break down
the day after the warranty has expired.

Himbrace

(him' bray s) n.
The strange hugging stance adopted by pairs
of Australian men, whereby they connect
their upper bodies, while leaving a good
half-metre of suspicion-free space between
their groins.

Hinterloper

(hin ta' low pa') n.

An Australian male who carries on like he's from the bush — wearing an Akubra hat, moleskins and a Driza-Bone — even though he's never been out of Paddo or St Kilda.

Hobarter

(ho' baa tah) v.

To fantasise about how much money you'd make if you swapped your overpriced house in Sydney or Melbourne for one of the cheap ones in Hobart, as pictured each week in the *Good Weekend*.

Holihads

(ho lee' hads) n.

The crumpled baggage tags from past holidays that you leave on your luggage so that others may know you once visited Paris.

Hope couture

(howp' ku toor) n.

The item of clothing you keep around for years in the vain hope you might fit back into it some day.

Dagword by Helen Lalas from a definition by Patricia McMillan. Also: Ought couture (Matthew O'Dempsey); Wishfits (Mel Dickson); Figgarments (Julie Horne); Hope-a-dashery (Garth Clarke); and Martin-Luthers (Mary and her friend Leanne), because, like Martin Luther King, they look into their cupboards and say, 'I have a dream'.

Hophazard

(hop' haz ad) n.

A solitary shoe or boot spotted lying in the middle of the road, with no explanation of what happened to its twin.

Hoptimistic

(hop tee' mis tik) adj.

To keep checking the fridge, late at night, in the belief that a final can of beer must be hiding in there somewhere.

Horrorgami

(hor ah' gah mee) n.
The vain attempt to re-fold a road map back the way it came, especially in high wind or while still driving.

Hurriclean

(hu ree' kleen) n.
The frenzied clean-up that occurs when you learn that you are having an important visitor at short notice.

Dagword by Michael Kennedy from a definition by Wendy Prior. Also: VIP-around (Ralph Belshaw); Fling-clean (Scott Watson); Sprung-clean (Carmelle Spiro); Demesstication (Rosie Langley); Cleanado (Narelle Darcy); and Glamourflage (Garry Walsh).

Hymnpersonator

(him pur' sin ay tah) n.
A person who only goes to church once a year, and doesn't know the words to the hymns, but still mugs along as if they're singing.

Hypocritic

(hip o' cri tik) n.

A film reviewer who says great things about bad films, just so they'll be quoted on the movie poster.

Ii

Ignominious rock
(ig noh' me ni us' rok) n.
The rock that's always under the place you've decided to hammer in your tent peg.

I-jacking
(eye' ja king) n.
The practice of following a conversation in order to spot the moment when you can jump in and make it all about yourself.

Dagword by Phil Sellen. Also: Mevesdropping (Curtis Ruhnau); Waitwatching (Michelle McDonald); and Converstalking (James Tulip).

Ike-oh
(eye key' oh) n.
The bolt or screw strangely left over after you've assembled your Ikea furniture.

Infiction

(in fik' shun) n.
Any infection or disease made up to avoid work or school.

Inhowlation

(in how lay' shun) n.
The terrifying intake of breath taken by a child before he or she cries.

Dagword by Barbara Maher from a definition by Julie Glasson. Also: Lull-a-bawl (Julie Grindrod); Precurser (Kate Kilpatrick); Pre-hysteric period (Ivan Hess); Breath Knell (Jo Hubble); Waitawail (Liz Holland); and Criatus (Kurt Douglas). Phrases: Pre-wailing winds (Colleen Rivers); Wait for rage (Patrick Ryan).

Jj

Jailopy
(jay lop' ee) n.
A flash sports car driven by someone so young, they just must be a drug dealer or dodgy entrepreneur.

Jetiquette
(jet' ee ket) n.
The etiquette expected when flying, whereby one should share the armrest with the person in the next seat, and at the same time refrain from falling asleep on their shoulder, dribbling.

Jobsconder

(job skon' dah) n.

A person who always disappears when there is work to be done.

Dagword by Andrew Harper from a definition by David Knight. Also: Evapor-mate (Julie Sanders); Taskvader (Garry Barbuto); Boltergeist (Bill Shannon); Offslider (Susan Bee); Helpulator (Wendy Pryor); and a Shwirker (Gillian Bullock).

Kk

Keyambulate
(kee am' bew layt) v.
To wear a bunch of keys on one's belt so as to prove one has large property investments, or at very least, a friend at Mister Minit.

Kindecision
(kin' dis i' jhun) n.
A feeling of uncertainty about which member of your extended family is actually the worst.

Kindyscretion

(kin dee' skre shun) n.

The loud, inappropriate, but usually truthful comment that your child makes at the worst possible moment. For example, 'Why is that man's bottom so big?' or 'Why is that lady dressed like a clown?'

Dagword by Eve Medina from a definition by Pierre Geromboux. Also: Braticism (Matthew O'Dempsey); Totshot (Shelley Warren); Babestruth (Barbara Maher); Cribtique (Annemarie Digby-Jones); and a Junior moment (Barry Simpson).

Kleptodialectic

(klep toh' dy a lekt' ik) adj.

Tending to copy the accent of whomever you are talking to, by turns becoming southern American, upper-class British, Hungarian...

Knack-nicker

(nak' nik ah) n.

A person who cannot leave a hotel room without taking every tea bag, sugar sachet, complimentary shampoo and even the spare loo roll.

Dagword by Tony Williams from a definition by Sue Gregory. Also: Complementarian (Frank Sehlmeier); Suite Sweeper (Chris Mahoney); Horderculturalist (Ben Little); Keptomaniac (Alison Anderson); Shampoachers (Kaye Osborn); Sampilferer (Steve Harop); Klepto-marriott (Simon Gregory); Shangri-larcenist (Barry Joseph);Travelooter (Tim Berthet); and Artful lodger (Dennis Shaw).

Kneerotica

(nee' rot ee kah) n.

The practice of touching knees with another person in a cinema or beneath a restaurant table in order to signal your romantic availability.

Kung-flu

(kung' floo) n.

A verbal battle between husband and wife over whose cold or flu is the worse, and thus who should be mollycoddled by the other.

L l

Laxicographer

(laks ik' og ra fah) n.

Someone who takes liberties with the language in order to make up words for the Dag's Dictionary.

Leer-mark

(leer' mahk) n.

The crease in the spine of a racy novel, indicating the rudest page.

Dagword by Wendy Hoving. Also: Onetrackspine (Luke Bradstreet); Bonkmark (David Schwartz); and Boobytrap (Ian Gorry).

Liebry

(ly' bree) n.

A pile of unread but fashionable books placed on a coffee table in order to impress visitors.

Limbpediments

(lim ped' ee ments) n.

The tangle of legs you must negotiate in order to get to take your seats at a sports match or concert.

Linge

(linj) n.
The mixture of lint, paperclips, loose change and pieces of Lego that can be found down the back of every lounge suite.

Lobotanist

(lob ot' an yst) n.
A person who can't even keep indoor plants alive.

Dagword by Bruce Reardon from a definition by David Doyle. Also: Brownthumb (Mary Werkhoven); Necroplanter (Greg Evans); and Osama bin garden (Neil Montgomery).

Lockade

(lok' ayd) n.

The wall of people with big hair who invariably sit right in front of you at the movies.

Lollycoddle

(loh lee' cod uhl) v.

During a long drive, to mollify children in the back seat of a car by throwing them regular supplies of junk food.

Loofrillys

(loo' fril eez) n.

Any craft object made as decoration for a bathroom, especially those designed to dispense any form of tissue.

Lopfooted

(lop' foo tid) adj.

Descriptive of a kid whose sandshoes are bigger than his head.

Lovestuck

(luhv' stuk) n.

The delicious but agonizing moment on a first date when both people *want* to make a move, but are scared of getting a knockback, and as a result nothing happens.

Dagword by Linda Krestensen from a definition by Miranda Bandler. Also: Pass-tense (Margo Reid); Lusterflies (Chris Kottaras); Pre-sensual tension (Nicole Goodwin); Ankissipation (Sue Berglund); Fore-pray (Allan Morris) and Great sexpectations (Judy Oliver).

Lurge

(lurj) n.

The confusing area where two street maps join, in which are located all parks, halls and other addresses.

Mm

McFamished
(mak' fam ishd) adj.
The feeling of being intensely hungry ten minutes after you've finished a meal at McDonald's.

McGuire

(ma' gwy ah) n.

When sitting around a smoky campfire, the really annoying eddy that is always in your face.

Dagword by Pip Denton, from a definition by George Czender.

Male-adjusted

(mayl' ad jus tid) adj.

Pertaining to the male belief that the more of the product you use the better will be the result, whether it's washing powder, shampoo or Viagra.

Maleodorous

(ma lee ow' duh rus) adj.

Descriptive of a car full of teenage boys on the way home from football training.

Malepractice

(mayl' prak tis) n.

The male inability to read an instructional manual until *after* they have started up the new appliance and broken it.

Malladroit

(mawl a' droyt) adj.

Descriptive of a person who gets hopelessly confused trying to work out the layout of a modern shopping mall.

Mallinger

(mawl ling' gah) v.

When young, to hang around a shopping mall for hours on end.

Manjar

(man' jah) n.

The jar, cup or bowl full of coins that is located somewhere in every man's bedroom.

Mansoon

(man' soon) n.
The sharp intake of breath when a young woman passes a group of business guys, and they all suck in their stomachs.

Mapparition

(map a' ri shun) n.
The spooky run of green lights you get whenever you desperately need to stop the car and consult a map.

Mashticate

(mash' ti kayt) v.
To use mashed potato as a means of capturing and consuming any peas left on your plate.

Mateneering

(mayt' en ear ing) n.
The competition between two men to climb to the top of anything.

Mergeician

(merj' i shun) n.

The rare person who stops and lets you into a stream of traffic, making a space suddenly appear out of nowhere.

Dagword by Alison Whittingham from a definition by Pip Greathead. Also: Wayfairer (Chris Klein); Hood samaritan (Tristan Harris); Motor Teresa (Phil Sellen); Road scholar (Grahame Windred); Sweet torquer (Jannine Hayek); Indicaterer (Cath Simpson); and a Tourist (Paul Springett).

Messpionage

(mess' pee on arj) n.

The examination of a young man's apartment by a new girlfriend in search of clues as to his character.

Micropest

(my cro' pest) n.

Any irritating animated figure that appears on your computer screen to offer help.

Minotouring
(my no' taw ring) v.
Being forced to navigate a labyrinth of ropes
or metal barriers at an airport or a bank, even
though you're the only customer in sight.

Moaner Leaser
(mo na' lee sah') n.
A renter, unhappy with her lot.

Moanologue

(mown o' log) n.

A lengthy speech about one's own failings designed to bring forth compliments, especially in relation to the meal you've just cooked.

Moanotone

(mown o' toen) n.

The faltering, beleaguered voice you put on when you ring into work to tell them you're sick.

Dagword by Judy Maynard from a definition by Peter Willey. Also: Malingua cranka (Sasa Kennedy); Slackcent (Tom Browell); Arggghccent (Joe Wickert); Sickliloquy (Nellie Evans); Flu'setto (John Sibbald); Phlegmbellishment (Richard Murnane); and Sicko voce (Dave Grinter). Phrases: a Hoarse whisperer (Paddy Mullin).

Mock-raker

(mok' ray kah) n.

Someone who constantly retells a story that makes you look like a goose.

Nn

Naggles
(naglz) n.
The well-worn belt holes, to the right of that currently in use, which reveal how much fatter you've become over the lifetime of the belt.

Nannasecond
(na na' sek und) n.
The split second between a child's arrival at their grandmother's and the provision of lollies and treats.

Narcolapse

(nar ko' laps) n.
The brilliant idea that comes to you in the
middle of the night, but by morning appears
to be the dumbest idea ever.

*Dagword by Laurent Rivory from a definition by
Carmel Summers. Also: Wiltergeist (Dianne Jameson);
Epiphony (Walter de Jong); and a Dimspiration
(Elizabeth Moore).*

Narcoplectic
(nar ko' plek' tic) adj.
Descriptive of the ill will felt by a sleepless person towards his or her happily snoring partner.

Navel-grazer
(nay vuhl' gray zah) n.
A young women attempting to eat as little as possible in the hope that she may show off her midriff by next summer.

Newslip
(newz' lip) n.
On a delivered newspaper, the edge of the plastic wrapper which must be located before the paper can be unrolled and read, by which time all the news is old.

Nicatosis
(nik a' toh sis) n.
The bad breath of cigarette smokers.

Nigglomaniac

(nig lo' may' nee ak) n.

A person who watches or nags you while you are attempting to do something, such as change a light bulb or reverse park a car — with the result that everything goes wrong.

Dagword by Cindy Alice from a definition by Paddy Mullin. Also: Hexpert (Mark Booth); Snoopervisor (Rob Cummins); Snipervisor (Jennifer Martin); and Spooktator (Philip Brain).

Nissanthropic

(nis an' thro pik) adj.

Descriptive of someone who hates people who drive Nissan Patrols.

Nom de womb

(nom' de woom) n.

A nickname for a baby while still in utero.

No-natal misconception

(no nay tul' mis kon sep' shun) n.
Any statement of congratulations given to a woman on account of her clearly pregnant belly, when in fact she's just put on a bit of weight.

Nonna

(no' na) n.
The missing ingredient in recipes handed down in Italian and Greek families, removed on purpose so that subsequent generations will never be able to make the dish quite as well as the grandmother.

Oo

One-upsonship
(won up' sun ship) n.
The nauseating fashion in which parents boast about their son's achievements, especially to people with a son the same age. *See also* one-updaughtership, one-upcarship, one-upgolfship.

Oodumboodumboodia
(oo dum' oo dum' oo dee ah) n.
The sense of panic that strikes Sydneysiders when trying to decide how many 'O's to include in the spelling of Woolloomooloo.

Ophthalparanoia
(op thal' pah rah noy' ah) n.
The belief, as you get older, that people are deliberately printing books and product instructions using smaller and smaller type, probably just to annoy you.

Oodumboodumboodia

Pp

Pantsformation

(pants' for may' shun) n.
The ability of a pair of pants to transmogrify into something hideous, and the wrong size, once you get them home from the shop.

Pantswipe

(pants' wyp) n.
The action by which you dry your hands on the back of your pants after using an electric hand-drying machine.

Paparatio

(pa pa' ray she oh) n.
The tendency for a Hollywood marriage to last in inverse proportion to the number of paparazzi covering the wedding ceremony.

Pastacarcerated

(pas ta' car sa ray' tid) adj.

For one's mouth to be firmly tied to one's plate by multiple strands of spaghetti, none of which will agree to be sucked up.

Peek-a-boo-boo

(peek' ah boo boo) n.

The act of pulling a cute, funny face at a baby in the supermarket queue, thus causing it to cry.

Peeking duck

(pee' king duk) n.

At a party, the act of constantly looking around the shoulder of the person you are talking to, in the hope of spotting someone more interesting.

Peerouette

(peer' oh ett) n.

The sudden movement that occurs when you are having a good perv at someone, and get caught, and so try to redirect your gaze as if you were in fact studying something just to the person's left or right.

Dagword by Michael Kennedy from a definition by Darren Spies. Also: Eye-vasion (J O'Shea); Eyeskating (Steve Harop); Eyejump (Barbara Maher); and Eyerobics (Craig Middleton).

Perfortify

(per for' tee fy) v.

The strange phenomenon whereby a paper product, such as a stamp or a cheque, appears to have been strengthened along the perforated lines, so that they are absolutely the last place that will ever tear.

Perfplume

(perf' ploom) n.

The wave of perfume that sweeps over you in the wake of an overdressed woman.

Phony tail

(fo nee' tayl) n.

The bit of hair grown longer by a bald man, so he can comb it over his bald patch.

Pieangulation

(pi' an gew lay' shun) n.

The constant changes of angle made by a meat pie-eater in order to keep the contents from spilling everywhere.

Piece de resistance

(pees' d re zis tonts) n.

The last bit of food left on a plate because everyone wants to be polite.

Dagword by Frances Rand from a definition by Greg Arrow. Also: Lingerfood (Peter Butterworth); A Remorsel (Richard Murnane); and Gluttanot (Mark O'Flynn). Phrase: Remains of the tray (Kim Smee).

Pinnumerate

(pin' new mer ayt) adj.

Descriptive of the point at which you have to remember so many different PINs for your bank account, computer, video store and Frequent Flyer Club, that you can't remember any.

Pisspoortraiture

(pis paw' trit cha) n.

The art practised by the chemist shop photographer when taking passport shots, whereby everyone looks like a drug runner.

Pistolation

(pis tol' ay shun) n.

The ability of a five-year-old boy to turn any object, however unlikely, into a gun.

Polephonist

(powl' foe nist) n.

A person who insists on pressing the button at the pedestrian crossing over and over again, even though once is quite enough.

Dagwood by Dave Cahill from a definition by Nerida White. Also: Manic depresser (Dennis Shaw); A cross presser (Richard Murnane); Presperado (Arwen Ximenes); Pressidivist (Frank Fitzgerald); Pressimist (Bev Paton); and Pressbuttonarian (Catherine Gray).

Pollicy

(pol' li cee) n.

Any political policy released during an election campaign, and therefore not to be believed.

Polyfester

(po lee fes' tah) n.

The smell produced when a lift full of business guys are wearing polyester shirts in summer.

Poultrygeist

(pol tree' guyst) n.
Any scary man dressed up in a chicken suit.

Pramdextrous

(pram deks' trus) adj.
Possessing the ability to both put up and collapse a modern pram without any industrial accidents.

Prawnography

(prorn og' rafee) n.

The enticing, full-colour photos of the Friday seafood buffet, as displayed in every RSL club foyer.

Proxymoron

(prok see' maw ron) n.

A person who always agrees with the chairman, the boss or any other leader.

Qq

Queuecumbered
(kew' kum burd) adj.
To be trapped in a queue which slowed down the instant you joined it.

Quizotic
(kwiz' otic) adj.
Compelled to shout answers towards a TV or radio whenever a quiz show is being broadcast, in the unrealistic belief you'd easily win.

Rr

Refridgermate
(re frij' a mayt) n.
A friend who only likes you for your cold beer.

Rollcalcitrance
(rowl' kal' see trants) n.
The male inability to put a new toilet roll on the holder, instead just propping it atop the cistern.

Dagword by Jo Brown. Also:
Unrolliability (Jo Kennedy); and
Spoolitis (Jennifer Wenden). Phrases:
The Patriarchal cistern.

Rumpage
(rump' ayg) n.
The amount of bum-cleavage on display in a woman's hipster pants.

Ss

Sadvertising
(sad' ver ty zing) n.
Any attempt to sell a product by preying
on the public's insecurities, particularly via
suggestions you may suffer from body odour,
bad breath or unattractive buttocks.

St Otis's dance
(saynt' ow tis iz' dans) n.
The lewd and crazy dance that you do when
alone in an elevator.

Santamonious
(san ta' mow nee us) adj.
Descriptive of the superior attitude adopted
by relatives who bought all their Christmas
presents at the half-yearly sales in July.

Saturday-morning-Disney, A

(sah ta' day maw' ning diz nee, a) n.

Any sexual position designed so that a couple may spring apart, and claim nothing was going on, should early morning TV fail to distract those children sharing the household.

Scamnesia

(skam' nee zia) n.

The curious ability to be fooled all over again when you get the envelope saying 'You Have Already Won a Prize in Our Million-Dollar Lottery'.

Scrankins

(skran' kinz) n.

The stale cereal in the bottom of the box that someone is forced to eat before a fresh box may be opened.

Scrubterfuge

(skrub' ta fewj) n.

A stratagem whereby teenagers remove any telltale signs of a party in the ten minutes before their parents get home.

Shampooeuse

(sham poo' us) n.

Someone who can sing beautifully, but only when under the shower.

Shankilate

(shank' e layt) v.

To regulate one's body heat during summer by sticking one leg out from under the doona.

Shinjuries

(shin' jur ees) n.

The multiple bruises, grass stains and tiny abrasions on the legs of a school kid.

Shinterjection

(shin' tah jek' shun) n.

At a dinner party, or in a business meeting, the sharp kick under the table that you give your partner to indicate that whatever he or she is saying, they must stop saying it right now.

Dagword by Mike Hluchan from a definition by Vivian Cassar-Patty. Also: Shin dig (Joan Currie); Toed rage (Barry Cranston); Drop-it kick (Robin King) and Shin bin (Denis Carnahan).

Showerdune

(showa' dyoon) n.
The shifting hillocks of sand in the bottom of a shower recess being used by beach goers.

Shyatus

(shy' ay tus) n.
The painful gap in conversation at the start of a dinner party, before the wine has kicked in.

Sighchological warfare

(sy' ko lo gee kal war' fare) n.

The practice, between a married couple, of letting loose a sigh of displeasure that is just loud enough for the partner to hear, but subtle enough that it can be denied if called to account.

Signlapses

(syn' lap sis) n.

Any error of punctuation or grammar found on a shop sign. In particular, quote marks used in the mistaken belief that they add emphasis, rather than an element of doubt, as in the phrases 'fresh' food, 'quality' ingredients and 'hygienic' kitchen.

Silicon valet

(silee kon' va lay) n.

A plastic surgeon who is at the constant beck and call of a Hollywood star.

Sillystine

(si lee' styn) n.

A person who refuses to acknowledge the considerable attractions of mindless pop culture, whether it be trashy magazines, Robbie Williams or romantic comedies.

Silicon valet

Sinband

(sin' band) n.

The band of pale skin found on a middle-aged man's ring finger, just after he's removed his wedding ring in the vain hope of appearing single.

Sirsatz

(sir' sats) n.

The overwhelming feeling of being a fake and a pretender experienced by an Australian bloke whenever a waiter calls him 'sir'.

Sitcombobulation

(sit com' bob u lay' shun) n.

The confusion experienced when you realise that, despite having watched only a handful of episodes of a particular sit-com, the episode they've chosen to repeat is always one you've seen three times before.

Skulldrudgery

(skul' drud jah' ree) n. '

Once you've shaved your head, the need to keep shaving so people don't realise you're trying to hide a bald spot.

Slightseer

(slyt' see ah) n.

A person who sees criticism in everything that's said to them.

Slobstacle

(slob' sta kuhl) n.

A person who just sits there as you try to vacuum or sweep around his or her feet.

Sloodge

(sloodj) n.

The soggy mash of food, sports clothes and notes from the teacher found in the bottom of a primary child's school bag.

Smugmelier

(smug' me lee ah) n.

Any waiter, but most commonly a wine waiter, who lords it over the customer.

Snackapop

(snak' a pop) n.

The sound made by a chip packet when you push in on the sides until the top bursts open with a satisfying pop.

Snackastrophe

(snak as' tro fee) n.

The tendency, when attempting a snackapop, for it to be the bottom seal of the packet that gives in first, thus depositing the chips all over your shoes.

Snaggle

(snag' gul) n.

The fifth and final sausage that you really shouldn't eat, but always do.

Snickerphant

(snik a' fant) n.

The person in the office who always laughs at the boss's jokes, however lame.

Snidge

(snidj) n.

The one dark sock that always smuggles itself into an all-whites wash.

Snock

(snok) n.

A sock that has lost its partner.

Snock pit

(snok' pit) n.

The pile of unpartnered socks kept at the bottom of the laundry basket, just in case the partners turn up.

Snoregasm

(snaw' gaz um) n.

The particularly delicious and abandoned moment experienced after you've pressed the snooze button on your alarm clock.

Soakosis

(sowk' oh sis) n.

The dangerous delusion, experienced while dreaming, in which you imagine yourself entering a bathroom and preparing for a much-needed wee. In nearly all cases you'll wake up in time.

Spewce

(spyuws) n.
The bright-red, about-to-be-sick colour that forty-year-old men go after playing squash.

Spilge

(spilj) n.
The yucky crust that forms around the top of a tomato sauce bottle.

Spoces

(spo' sez) n.
The dozen jars of expired Indian spices and chutneys located at the very back of your cupboard from the one time you tried to cook a curry.

Spudbodgie

(spud' bod gee) n.
The blackened bad chip included in every order of fish and chips.

Spuddle

(spuh dhul) n.
The puddle of butter atop a jacket potato.

Staralysis

(stah' a lee sis) n.
The peculiar paralysis that overcomes even quite normal people when in the presence of a film star.

Suffermore

(suf ah' moor) n.
A person who is always sicker or worse off than you. If you say you are a bit tired, they are exhausted. If you're sick, they're on death's door. If you're snowed under with work they say something like 'Try doing it with six children'. And when someone runs up the back of your car, it's nothing compared to the accident they had in the summer of '84.

Dagword by Susan Bee from a definition by Felicity Barclay. Also: Sickerchondriac (Wendy Pryor); a Hurtuoso (Jenny Lowe); Sickophant (Lloyd Capps); Moanarchist (Arthur Lathouris); and a Painsayer (Richard Murnane).

Sussphisticate

(sus' fis' tee kate) n.

The mythical friend of your child whose
parents supposedly permit all the things
your child is banned from doing.

Swiggel

(swi' guhl) v.
To swap your socks around so the holes are no longer aligned with your big toes.

Swigmata

(swig' mah tah) n.
The red marks that form on the nose and cheeks after a night of heavy drinking.

Tt

Taggadocio

(tag' ah doe' she oh) n.
Vain, empty boasting by means of wearing clothes with a visible brand name.

Tag-snatch

(tahg' snach) v.
To slyly grab a look at someone's name-tag at an official function, to hide the fact that you have forgotten their name.

Tanti-climax

(tan tee' cly max) n.
The bit when the toddler throws himself face-forward on the supermarket floor and holds his breath.

Taskquerade

(tars kuh' rayd) n.

A bunged-on, 'gee-I'm-busy' activity that is commenced the instant the boss walks near your desk, and relinquished the moment he or she leaves the vicinity.

Tearerist

(te rah' ryst) n.

A person in a cinema who seems to take ages to unwrap their lollies or open their chips, then eats them one by one, oblivious to the noise.

Dagword by Barry Cranston from a definition by Nicholas Pyne. Also: A Cellopain (Christopher Stollery); a Roxymoron (Dennis Shaw); IMAX-ticator (Jeff Pross); and a Tornmenter (Andrew Newman). Phrases: A Weapon of multiplex distraction (James Gallagher); the Man from la muncha (Steve Harop).

Tel-Dorado

(tel' dor ah' doh) n.

A mythical city where companies get humans to answer their phones.

Tele-phony
(tell e' fon ee) n.
On the phone, the recorded voice that tells you to wait for an hour on hold because 'your business is important to us'.

Testiculation
(tes tik' yu lay' shun) n.
The male habit of giving one's testicles a quick squeeze or prod at three-minute intervals throughout the working day, just to check they haven't suddenly disappeared, or been pecked off by wild birds.

Textibitionist
(teks ti bi' shun ist) n.
Someone who shows they are young and groovy by writing ordinary snail mail letters in text-message style. Don't you h8 them?

Thingdignation

(thing dig nay' shun) n.

Anger or scorn aroused by an inanimate object which refuses to work, usually leading to the use of phrases such as 'Work, damn you', 'This is your last chance', and 'Tell me what I've ever done to you?'

Thinges

(thin' jes) n.

The thin plastic hinges on a CD box, which inevitably break within moments of purchase.

Thinstructor

(thin struk' tah) n.

A person hired by a gym to be an inspiration to us all.

Thinsult

(thin' sult) n.

Behaviour exhibited by slim, diet-conscious people when they pat their flat stomachs and lament how 'appallingly fat' they are in front of their much fatter friends.

Thumbdriver

(thum' dry vah) n.

The name given to your thumb when it's being used to tighten the tape on a video.

Tidge

(tidj) n.

The two centimetres of red wine you leave in the bottle overnight in order to demonstrate to your partner, and to yourself, that you are not a complete alcoholic.

Tiechosis

(ty' ko sis) n.
An affliction whereby a person wears a cartoon-character tie in a futile attempt to appear amusing.

Tightwadelaidian

(tyt wod a lay' dee an) n.
A person who fantasises about driving all the way to Adelaide just to cash in the five cents refund offered on their soft-drink bottle.

Timtamper

(tim' tam' puh) v.
To cannily open a packet of Tim Tams, remove a biscuit, and then slide back the plastic sleeve, hoping no-one will notice.

Tisme

(tis' me) n.
A person who begins a phone conversation saying, 'It's me', then gets offended when you don't recognise their voice.

Toastankerous

(towst' tan ker us) adj.
Characteristic of a toaster that, while on the same setting, will undercook the first slice of bread, then burn the second.

Todknackering

(tod' nak er ing) n.

The phenomenon whereby a three year old, running joyfully towards his or her father, will be the perfect height to head-butt the father in the testicles. Opinions differ as to whether this is accidental, or a very advanced form of sibling rivalry, ensuring a new sibling will never even be conceived.

Tollings

(tolings) n.
The scattered coins that can be found beneath the seat of every car, left over from the process of paying the toll.

Toothbrash

(tooth' brahsh) adj.
Pertaining to the new generation of toothbrushes that have so many grip panels and anti-slip surfaces, you'd think you were piloting a fighter jet.

Torge

(torj) n.
The tall, handsome man at a party who always turns out to be a complete bastard.

Tortune

(tor' tyoon) n.

A catchy, yet awful song that you just can't get out of your head for days, even after hearing it played just once on the radio.

Dagword by Mark Glass from a definition by Barbara Farrelly. Also: An Irritune (Donna Churchland); an ABBAration (David Potter); Regurgitrack (Peter Owens); Popstickle (Mick Everett); Recalcichant (Frank Sehlmeir); or a Minogue (Beccy Connell) — since 'I just can't get you out of my head.'

Toupee-coupe

(too' pay koo' pay) n.

A flash sports car driven by a middle-aged man.

Traince

(tray' nts) n.

The strange quiet after a train has stopped between stations and all the passengers look upwards, wondering whether the stop will be for twenty seconds or five hours.

Transvegetation

(trans' vej ee tay' shun) n.

The tendency for pieces of carrot to suddenly appear when people throw up, even when the person hasn't eaten carrot for years.

Tupperburp

(tup ah' berp) v.

To expel the air from a plastic food container in the belief that this will somehow help keep things fresh.

Twingest

(twin' jest) adj.

The predisposition to use twice the quantity of any product, once you know it's the diet or lite version.

Uu

Undie-performer
(undee' pur for mah) n.
A person who believes they will not pass their exams unless they are wearing their lucky undies.

Undie-statement
(undee' stayt ment) n.
Any underwear designed to be worn with the brand name showing.

Unexpectorate
(un' eks pek' tor ayt) v.
To dribble sudsy toothpaste onto one's own chin, in a failed attempt to spit it into the basin.

Upendectomy

(up' end ek' tom ee) n.

A process by which funfair operators earn coins and other valuables by turning their customers upside down, and giving them a good shake.

Vv

Valenteenies

(valen tee' neez) n.

Minuscule scraps of transparent cloth given by a man to his wife or girlfriend on Valentine's Day, in the hope that she will be tricked into thinking it is actually a present for her.

Vegemate

(veggy' mayt) n.

An Australian pal who sends you supplies of Vegemite while you are overseas.

Verboaster

(verb' ow stah) n.

A person who always uses a complicated and pretentious word when a simple one will do.

Dagword by Michael Kennedy from a definition by Sophie Scott. Also: Word smythe (Rob Cummins); Vocabulair (Michele Manz); Jargonaut (Scott Holmes); and a Lexicontortionist (Julie Ellis).

Veriflycation

(veri fly kay' shun) n.

That involuntary movement of checking the fly made by all men as they re-enter a public place after leaving the bathroom.

Dagword by Steven Winter from a definition by Melanie Bruce. Also: Flyby (Kara Ward); Zip-I-dee-did-I (Helen Richards); a Weeassurance (Maria Prendergast); Heflex action (Russell Ridgeway); and Penis fly tap (Raymond Lees). Phrase: 'Going to the video referee', as it involves checking the tackle is legal (Greg Wall).

Vidiot

(vid'ee ut) n.

A person who hires the same movie they borrowed from the video store last week, having completely forgotten the experience.

I've seen this.

Vodge

(vodj) v.

To stare vacantly at your computer as it downloads a page from the Internet, transfixed by the progress of the download bar.

Voidcast

(voyd' kast) n.

Transmission from a TV or radio left on in an empty house to discourage thieves.

Voodoodle

(voo doo' duhl) v.

To wreak revenge on a politician by scribbling on his photograph in the paper, adding horns, fangs, a beard and spectacles.

Ww

Wasmosis
(was mo' sis) n.
The rule whereby every era of fashion, however ugly, finally works its way back to the top, and to a revival.

Wedgetarian
(wedj a' tayr' ee an) n.
A child whose diet consists solely of potato wedges, with occasional side-serves of chips.

Weeanderthal
(wee' and ah thal) n.
A suburban man who feels the need to express his primitive side by weeing in the backyard.

Weenertia

(wee' nur she ah) n.

The moment in the morning when you can't get out of bed, even though you urgently need a wee.

Weetreat, to beat a

(wee' treet, to beet a) v.

When at a party, to claim a sudden need to go to the bathroom, in order to escape further conversation with the most boring person there.

Weeanderthal

Whodle

(wo' duhl) n.

An all-purpose question asked at a party, such as, 'How's tricks?', 'What have you been up to?', designed to disguise the fact that you've entirely forgotten the person's name, occupation and personal history.

Widdlejig

(widuhl' jig) n.

The frantic dance done by a five year old when they want to go to the toilet, but haven't quite realised it.

Woofhead

(woof' hed) n.

A person whose hairstyle is modelled on that of their dog.

Wrapoplexy
(rap o' plek see) n.
The moment of panic experienced by a snack food consumer when they find themselves unable to tear or bite open the plastic wrapper.

Wreckfest
(rek' fest) n.
A disgusting fry-up breakfast eaten by someone with a hangover, in the hope of feeling vaguely human.

XLation
(ek sel ay' shun) n.
The grunt made by a fat man when he bends down to pick something up.

Yy

Yankcent

(yank' sent) n.

The bad American accent put on by Australians when they wish to portray somebody as loud and crass, whatever their actual nationality.

Yellephonist

(yel e' fon ist) n.

A person on a train or bus who is talking loudly on their mobile phone, content to reveal the most intimate details of their private lives for everyone to hear.

Dagword by Graeme Levy from a definition by Tanya Neill. Also: Trainsbitionist (Jeanette Dibden); Nymphonemaniac (Julie King); and Airjacker (Steve Harop).

Yuckvangelist

(yuk van' gel ist) n.

A person who, after biting into something disgusting, encourages others to try it, just so they can appreciate how truly bad it is.

Yulelation

(yul' lay shun) n.

The very special feeling that comes when you know Christmas is over for another year.

Zz

Zebars

(ze bars) n.
The white stripes left on women's bodies after sunbathing in a bikini.

Zeitgust

(zyt' gust) n.
The wind that always comes up at the precise time you try to light a match.